CORNERSTONES OF FREEDOM™

ELLIS ISLAND

BY MELISSA McDANIEL

CHILDREN'S PRESS®
An Imprint of Scholastic Inc.
New York Toronto London Auckland Sydney
Mexico City New Delhi Hong Kong
Danbury, Connecticut

BRINGING HISTORY to LIFE

Content Consultant
Vincent Cannato, PhD
Associate Professor, Department of History
University of Massachusetts, Boston
Boston, Massachusetts

Library of Congress Cataloging-in-Publication Data
McDaniel, Melissa, 1964–
  Ellis Island/by Melissa McDaniel.
     p. cm.—(Cornerstones of freedom)
  Includes bibliographical references and index.
  ISBN-13: 978-0-531-25031-0 (lib. bdg.)   ISBN-10: 0-531-25031-8 (lib. bdg.)
  ISBN-13: 978-0-531-26556-7 (pbk.)   ISBN-10: 0-531-26556-0 (pbk.)
 1. Ellis Island Immigration Station (N.Y. and N.J.)—Juvenile literature.
2. United States—Emigration and immigration—History—Juvenile
literature. I. Title. II. Series.
  JV6484.M39 2011
  304.8'73—dc22   2011011310

1 2 3 4 5 6 7 8 9 10 R 21 20 19 18 17 16 15 14 13 12

Photographs © 2012: AP Images: 56 (George Brich), 55 (M. Spencer
Green), 57 (Marty Lederhandler), 24 (North Wind Picture Archives),
10, 59 top; Bridgeman Art Library International Ltd., London/New York/
Private Collection/Peter Newark American Pictures: 13; Getty Images:
14 (Fotosearch), 42 (MPI), 4 top, 28 (NY Daily News), 49 (Michael Ochs
Archives); Library of Congress: 15 top, 17, 30, 32, 58 (Bain News Service),
15 bottom (N. Currier), 11 (Currier & Ives), 25 (Edwin Levick), 41 (Al
Ravenna/New York World-Telegram & Sun Collection), 7, 16, 22 bottom,
33; Melissa McDaniel: 64; North Wind Picture Archives: 12; ShutterStock,
Inc.: 50 (Philip Lange), 59 bottom (Philip Lange); Superstock, Inc./Image
Asset Management Ltd.: 2, 3, 4 bottom, 8; The Granger Collection, New
York: 47 (F. Victor Gillam), cover, 51 (Lewis Hine), 36, 37 (Rue des Archives),
39 (ullstein bild), back cover, 5 left, 5 right, 21, 22 top, 23, 26, 31, 34, 38,
40, 44, 45, 46, 48; The Image Works: 20 (Mary Evans Picture Library), 18
(Roger-Violett).

Did you know that studying history can be fun?

BRING HISTORY TO LIFE by becoming a history investigator. Examine the evidence (primary and secondary source materials); cross-examine the people and witnesses. Take a look at what was happening at the time—but be careful! What happened years ago might suddenly become incredibly interesting and change the way you think!

Contents

In Search of a Better Life

In Europe during the 1800s, political, social, and economic problems caused millions of people to suffer terribly. In Ireland, crops failed and people starved in a widespread **famine**. All across the continent jobs and usable farmland were hard to find. Many people suffered religious and political **persecution** as well. In Russia and eastern Europe, governments carried out massacres called **pogroms**, intended to force Jewish people to flee. In Turkey, the government instituted programs to eliminate all Armenians living in the Turkish empire. Wars and revolutions left many people homeless and struggling to survive.

Across Europe, people searched for a glimmer of hope and a small chance to make a better life for themselves and their families. Many people thought those opportunities could be found in the United States of America. Europeans heard tales of people moving to America with nothing and becoming rich and successful.

"The streets are paved with gold," they were told. These promises of a better life in a faraway land prompted millions of Europeans to sail across the Atlantic Ocean in search of fulfilling their dreams.

"If America did not exist, we would have had to invent it for the sake of our own survival," said one Italian **immigrant**. And so a great migration to America began—a life-changing journey filled with hope and excitement.

Many people left Europe for the United States in the 19th century.

MOVED TO AMERICA BETWEEN 1871 AND 1940.

CHAPTER 1

COMING TO AMERICA

Most immigrants brought only a few possessions with them.

ON JANUARY 1, 1892, A YOUNG Irish girl named Annie Moore walked down a gangplank onto Ellis Island, in New York Harbor. It was her 15th birthday. Bells and whistles rang out, but not in her honor. Instead, the joyous noises were celebrating the first day of operation of the Ellis Island **Immigration** Station.

Annie was led into a large building at the center of the island and up to the registry desk. She was the first immigrant ever registered at Ellis Island. The commissioner of immigration presented her with a $10 gold coin and welcomed her to America, her new home.

Annie and her two younger brothers, ages 7 and 11, had spent 12 days at sea crossing the Atlantic Ocean. In New York City, they were reunited with their parents, who had come to the United States earlier. After the exhausting 3,000-mile (5,000 kilometer) journey, the children eagerly looked forward to building their new life in America.

YESTERDAY'S HEADLINES

On January 2, 1892, the *New York Times* reported the opening of the Ellis Island Immigration Station. The article began:

LANDED ON ELLIS ISLAND

NEW IMMIGRATION BUILDINGS OPENED YESTERDAY

A ROSY-CHEEKED IRISH GIRL THE FIRST REGISTERED

—ROOM ENOUGH FOR ALL ARRIVALS—

ONLY RAILROAD PEOPLE FIND FAULT

The new buildings on Ellis Island constructed for the use of the Immigration Bureau were yesterday formally occupied by the officials of that department. The employees reported at an early hour, and each was shown to his place by the Superintendent or his chief clerk. Col. Weber was on the island at 8 o'clock, and went on a tour of inspection to see that everything was in readiness for the reception of the first boatload of immigrants.

In the following decades, 12 million immigrants passed through Ellis Island, their hearts bursting with joy and fear, sadness about the homes they had left behind, and hope for the future.

The Changing Island

The small patch of land now called Ellis Island lies close to the coast of New Jersey. The Lenape Native Americans, who originally lived in the region, called it *Kioshk*, which means "gull island." The Dutch and English began arriving in the region in the 1600s, and they called it Little Oyster Island, because of its rich oyster beds. By 1765,

New York Harbor was one of the busiest ports in the country.

the island was used as a place to hang pirates. Because of this, it was renamed Gibbet Island, after the structure on which the pirates were hanged.

In the mid-1770s, a New York merchant named Samuel Ellis bought the island. He ran a tavern and a fish business on Ellis Island. In 1808—years after Ellis died—New York took over the island and then sold it to the

Little-used Ellis Island did not stand out in the busy harbor.

federal government. The government built **fortifications** there, making it part of a ring of forts that protected New York. In the following decades, the military stored gunpowder and other supplies on the island.

Over time, however, Ellis Island fell into disuse. The small island sat quiet amid the bustle of New York Harbor.

A Growing Nation

Early in the 1800s, an estimated 60,000 immigrants were arriving in the United States each decade. In the 1830s, the numbers grew significantly. Many of these people were Irish, who were fleeing hunger and desperate poverty back home. As the years rolled on, immigrants sailed from across the seas into Boston, Baltimore, Seattle, San Francisco, Savannah, and other cities. But the busiest port was New York City.

People from all around the world sailed into New York City.

Ships sailing from Europe to America were often very crowded.

During this period, anyone wanting to move to the United States merely had to arrive, and they were free to stay. No one questioned them upon their arrival. They walked off their ships onto American soil and into a new life.

Eventually, states began setting up receiving stations to deal with the rising tide of immigrants. In 1855, New York established the Castle Garden immigration station at the southern tip of Manhattan Island. People who arrived there could exchange money and get information about travel, jobs, and housing. Between 1855 and 1890, about eight million people passed through Castle Garden.

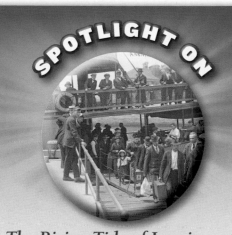

The Rising Tide of Immigrants

During the 1800s, the number of immigrants arriving in the United States soared. The following figures appear in the *Yearbook of Immigration Statistics,* published by the U.S. Office of Immigration Statistics in 2009.

Years	Number of Immigrants
1820–1829	128,509
1830–1839	538,381
1840–1849	1,417,337
1850–1859	2,814,554

Castle Garden was the main immigration station in New York City from 1855 to 1890.

Immigration officers checked new immigrants for signs of contagious diseases.

The U.S. Government Steps In

Some people opposed letting an unlimited number of immigrants enter the country. They asked the government to limit immigration. In 1891, the federal government officially took over the regulation of new arrivals by creating the Bureau of Immigration. Laws were passed that rejected immigrants with **contagious** diseases. People with disabilities that might make them unable to take care of themselves were also rejected.

A FIRSTHAND LOOK AT
A SHIP'S MANIFEST

Annie Moore was the first immigrant registered at the Ellis Island Immigration Station. Her name appears on the **manifest** of the *Nevada,* the ship that brought her to the United States. "Annie Moore" is written on the second line of the list, which also states her age as "13" (although she was actually 14 at the time) and notes that her destination is "New York." She was processed through Ellis Island on her 15th birthday. See page 60 for a link to view the handwritten passenger list.

A large inspection station was needed to enforce these rules. The government decided that Ellis Island would be an ideal site for the nation's first federal immigration station. By the following year, buildings had been constructed, and the "Island of Hope" was ready to greet Annie Moore and the millions of others who would follow.

The millions of immigrants who passed through Ellis Island brought greater diversity to the United States.

CHAPTER 2

A NEW LAND

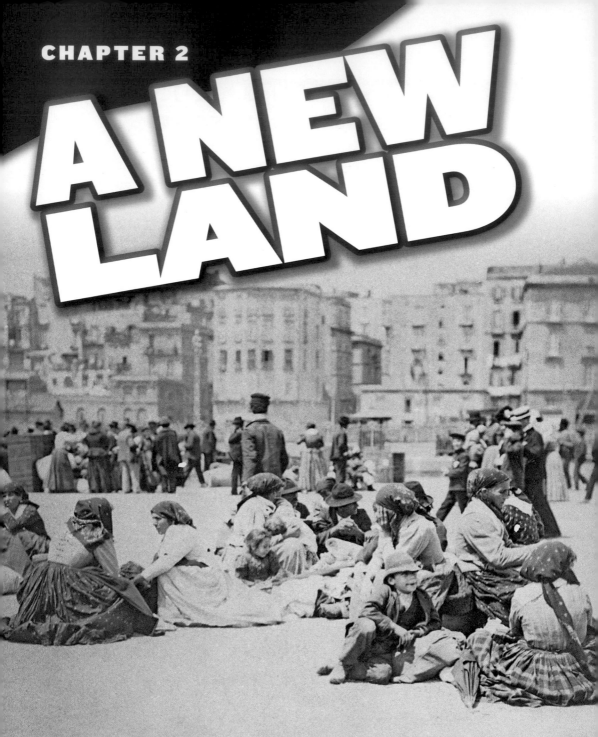

Italian immigrants take a final look at their home country while waiting for their ship to arrive.

MOVING TO AMERICA MEANT leaving the country where everyone spoke your language. It also meant leaving behind friends and family. After saying good-bye, immigrants were often unlikely to ever see their loved ones again. "Going to America then was almost like going to the moon," said Golda Meir, who moved from Russia to Wisconsin as a child and eventually became prime minister of Israel. "We were all bound for places about which we knew nothing at all and for a country that was totally strange to us."

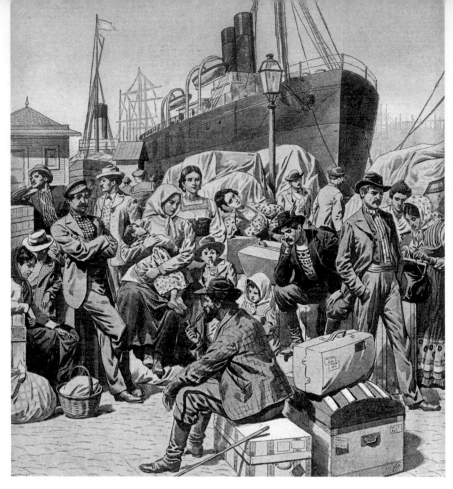

Immigrant families hoped for better lives in the United States.

The Journey Begins

Getting to America was a difficult task. People saved money, sometimes for years, to pay for the steamship ticket. Sometimes they sold almost everything they owned to raise money. Often, one member of a family would go to America first, in hopes of finding a job. That person would then send money to help bring the rest of the family over. When the family had enough money saved, they packed their bags and baskets. They brought just a few precious items—photographs, wedding dresses, musical instruments, family linens—and began their journey.

Most people lived far from the ports where the huge ships that would bring them across the ocean were docked. European immigrants streamed across the continent. They headed for major port cities such as Liverpool, England; Hamburg, Germany; and Naples and Genoa, Italy. The immigrants left their homes in Italy, Russia, Hungary, Germany, Turkey, and many other nations. They made their way to the ports in any way they could. Some walked, some rode in wagons, and some rode on trains. Many had never before ventured away from their small villages. They were truly heading into the unknown.

Most immigrants traveled to America on huge ships.

Home Countries

The immigrants who entered through Ellis Island came from everywhere—Scotland, Greece, Spain, Russia, Turkey, the West Indies, Canada. The largest numbers of immigrants to pass through Ellis Island were Italian. In total, 2,502,310 Italians entered. By 1908, there were 700,000 Italians living in New York City. At the time, the population of Rome, the capital of Italy, was only 500,000. The country that had the largest percentage of its people leave was Iceland. By 1914, one-fifth, or 20 percent, of the population of Iceland had left for North America.

Onto the Ship

Steamship companies inspected their passengers before they were allowed to board. They did this because if officials at Ellis Island rejected an immigrant, the company had to return the person to Europe at no cost to that person.

The steamship companies asked passengers their age, nationality, and occupation. They

Many immigrants came to New York from Italy.

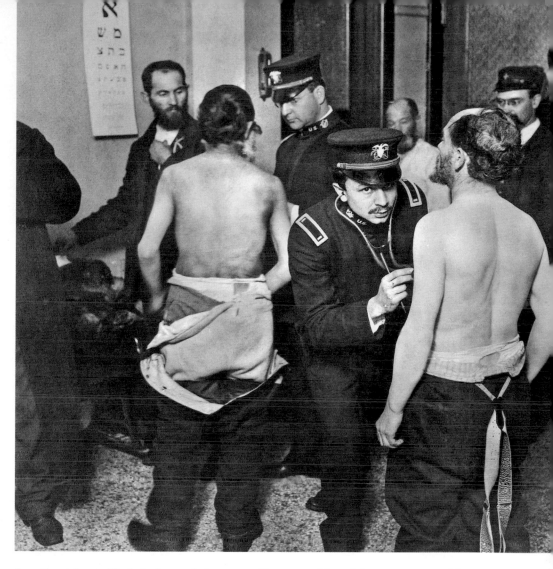

Immigration officials hoped that manifests and health exams would help with keeping diseases out of the United States.

asked if they could read and how much money they were carrying with them. This information was put on the ship's manifest. At Ellis Island, the information on the manifests helped determine whether people could enter the country. In later years, manifests also included information about immigrants' physical and mental health, and their political views.

People in steerage sections had to endure poor living conditions on their voyage.

The Crossing

Most steamships had three different types of tickets: first class, second class, and **steerage**. Passengers with first-class tickets slept in large cabins with comfortable beds and running water. Second-class passengers also got cabins, though they were smaller.

Steerage was the least expensive ticket. Most immigrants had little money, so about 90 percent of the people heading to Ellis Island were in steerage. Steerage was the lowest level of the boat. There were no cabins in steerage. Instead, there were only rows of bunks, and sometimes not even that.

Steerage conditions were often very poor. A thousand people could be packed into the steerage area. No fresh air made it into steerage, so the air was thick with foul odors. The food was barely edible, and the noise from the ship's engines was deafening.

During calm weather, steerage passengers spent as much time as they could on deck, breathing the clean, crisp sea air. But during storms, people had no choice but to return to the unpleasant steerage compartment, as the ship was tossed on the waves. "Oh, God, I was sick," recalled Bertha Devlin, an immigrant from Ireland. "Everybody was sick. I don't ever want to remember anything about that old boat."

Sometimes thousands of immigrants crowded onto each ship.

With people packed tightly together on the ships, disease spread quickly. So many people died that the immigrant ships were sometimes called coffin ships. If a person died during the crossing, the body was thrown overboard, to sink beneath the cold, dark waves.

The Welcoming Torch

Usually, after about two weeks at sea, the steamships would sail into New York Harbor. The passengers rushed to the ship's railings to catch their first glimpse of America.

The sight of the Statue of Liberty let the immigrants know that they had finally arrived in America.

Often, the first thing they saw was the Statue of Liberty. Passengers gaped at the towering statue of a woman holding a torch in the air. "Lady Liberty" served as a symbol of freedom, welcoming those fleeing persecution and hardship around the world. On the base of the statue is inscribed a poem by Emma Lazarus. It reads:

Give me your tired, your poor,
Your huddled masses yearning to breathe free,
The wretched refuse of your teeming shore.
Send these, the homeless, tempest-tost to me,
I lift my lamp beside the golden door!

As the ship continued on toward shore, the immigrants' hearts filled with joy. But before they could reach their future home, one last obstacle remained: they would have to pass through Ellis Island.

A FIRSTHAND LOOK AT
IMMIGRANTS AND THE STATUE OF LIBERTY

An immigrant from Poland remembered seeing the Statue of Liberty as the boat steamed into New York Harbor. He later said, "The bigness of Mrs. Liberty overcame us. No one spoke a word, for she was a goddess and we knew she represented the big, powerful country which was to be our future home." A sketch made in 1887 shows passengers aboard the steamship *Germanic* with the Statue of Liberty coming into view. See page 60 for a link to view the original illustration.

CHAPTER 3

ISLAND OF HOPE

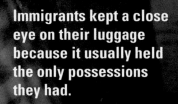

Immigrants kept a close eye on their luggage because it usually held the only possessions they had.

Newcomers to America

streamed off their ships. They were excited to be so close to their destination. But they were also fearful of their new surroundings, of losing their luggage, and of becoming separated from their family members. They were surrounded by a mass of people speaking languages they could not understand. The trip through Ellis Island was confusing and frightening. It could take a few hours—or months.

Off the Ship

The steamships pulled up to a pier in Manhattan. The first- and second-class passengers were inspected there, and then most were free to leave. Only those who were obviously sick or in legal trouble had to go to Ellis Island. Officials assumed that because these immigrants had enough money for an expensive ticket, they would be able to take care of themselves.

The steerage passengers and their few possessions were loaded onto a barge, which took them to Ellis Island. The first stop inside the main building was the

Most immigrants were glad to be back on solid ground after the long journey at sea.

Immigrants at Ellis Island left their luggage in piles, hoping it would still be there when they returned for it.

baggage room. Eleanor Lenhart, an immigrant from England, recalled a man "shouting at the top of his voice, 'Put your luggage here, drop your luggage here. Men this way. Women and children this way.' Dad looked at us and said, 'We'll meet you back here at this mound of luggage and hope we find it and you again.'"

The Medical Inspection

The medical exam was the first stop in the inspection. The main inspection was done as immigrants stood in a line. Immigrants walked single file past officials

Many immigrants were children.

and doctors, who looked for signs of illness, disease, or disability. They checked for limps, coughs, mental illness, and much more.

If a doctor suspected that there was something wrong with an immigrant, he would write a letter in chalk on the back of the person's coat. *L* stood for lameness, or difficulties with movement, *E* for eye problems, *X* for possible mental illness, and so on. The doctors in a later formal exam paid special attention to the concerns raised by the chalk marks.

It was said that doctors at Ellis Island could do the formal exam in just six seconds. They could tell whether an immigrant's heart was healthy from the color of the fingernails. They looked down throats. They made sure the newcomers could hear. Doctors also tested for a contagious eye disease called trachoma. Trachoma was one of the most common reasons why immigrants were refused entry into the United States.

There were often large numbers of people waiting to begin the process of examination.

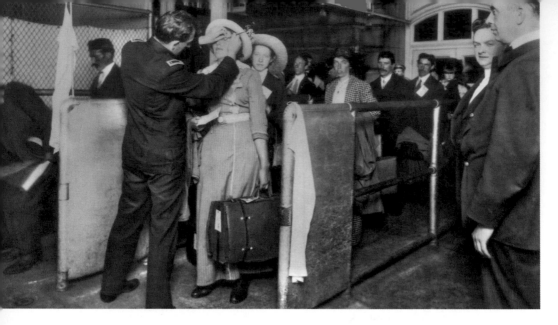

The medical inspection was an unpleasant part of the immigration process.

Anyone with a chalk mark had to go to a separate line for further inspection. Immigrants worried that their husbands and wives and children who faced closer inspection might be **deported**. They feared that if they were separated at Ellis Island, even for a moment, they might never see each other again. One young woman was terrified at the sight of a chalk mark on her little

A FIRSTHAND LOOK AT
AN EYE TEST

Red and watery eyes were signs that a newcomer had trachoma. To be certain, doctors performed what was known as the buttonhook test. The doctor turned the eyelid inside out using a tool called a buttonhook. Buttonhooks were normally used to fasten buttons on shoes. The test was painful, and immigrants dreaded it. See page 60 for a link to view a collection of buttonhooks used in eye exams.

sister's coat. The coat had a nice lining, and a stranger recommended that the little girl simply turn the coat inside out. She did, and she escaped the second inspection and perhaps being sent home.

Doctors gave people marked with an X—indicating a mental disability—an intelligence test. The test might be a jigsaw puzzle or a memory game. Some newcomers had trouble with these simple tests because they didn't speak English. Others were too tired, confused, or nervous to answer correctly.

A VIEW FROM ABRO★AD

Writer Isaac Bashevis Singer grew up in Poland and came to America in 1935. But in his youth, he often heard stories of people who had left for America and were turned away because of illness, especially trachoma. He recalled,

There was a great fear of this island because people were told that if the doctors find that someone is sick, they send him back. So many immigrants, I remember, before they went to America, went to doctors to cure their eyes and all kinds of sicknesses which they suspected might hinder them of entering the United States.

The Legal Inspection

Following the medical inspection, newcomers descended into the Great Hall, or Registry Room, for the legal inspection. The Great Hall was a grand room divided

The Great Hall was able to hold a huge number of people.

by iron railings, which made the room look like a giant cattle pen. It was loud and crowded, with people talking and shouting in dozens of different languages.

"The one thing I remember about Ellis Island was confusion," recalled Irish immigrant Thomas Rogen. "A lot of movement and people, women wearing kerchiefs and boxes and bundles. I remember . . . rows of benches in a big hall with kids running in all directions."

In the Great Hall, immigrants waited for their names to be called. When they heard their names, they would go to be interviewed by an immigration inspector. Interpreters helped the immigrants speak with the inspectors by translating languages for them.

The inspectors asked the newcomers many questions and checked the answers against the information that appeared on the ship's manifest. A wrong answer could lead to the immigrant being deported.

Immigrants were also asked how much money they had with them. For a brief time, a rule at Ellis Island said that each immigrant had to have $25 to enter the country. Today, that amount is roughly equal to $550. It was a large sum for a person who had just scraped together enough to buy a boat ticket. After an uproar about the rule, it was discontinued, but immigrants continued to believe they needed $25.

Immigrants were careful about how they answered the questions asked at Ellis Island.

Stuck on the Island

Most immigrants made it through the inspection in three to five hours. But others spent a much longer time on Ellis Island. Some who were sick were sent to hospital buildings on the island until they were better. Others were **detained** for a period of time for questioning. Sometimes this was because officials suspected they had extreme political views and might want to overthrow the U.S. government. Other times, it was because they did not have the skills to make a living in America.

Thousands of young women who came to America to get married were also detained at Ellis Island. Immigration officials sent a letter or a telegram to the man the woman was to marry, telling him to come to Ellis Island. The woman was not allowed to go ashore until her future husband came to claim her.

Detained immigrants were not allowed to enter the country until their issues were sorted out.

Detained immigrants lived in dormitories on the island.

Those who were detained spent night after night in bunks in dormitories, or separate buildings, on the island. "There were [people] who had been there for weeks and some for months, some as much as a year," says one man. "And there was a feeling of desperation because we had no idea when we would get out and neither did other people."

But most did get out. Each morning, officials read the names of those who were free to go. Cheers of support were given to the lucky ones. A few more immigrants had made it through the "Golden Door" into America.

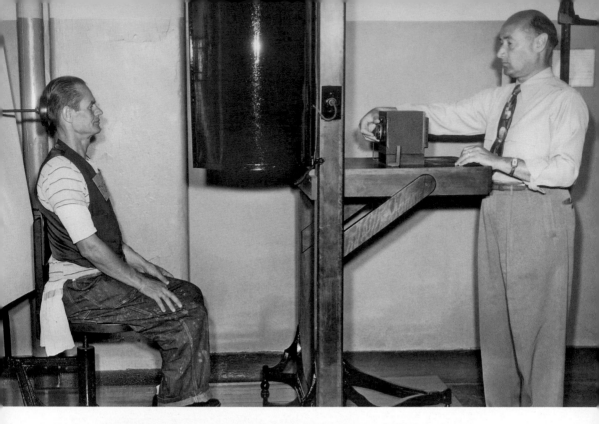

Immigrants were photographed before being deported.

Island of Tears

Not everyone was so lucky. About 2 percent of all immigrants did not pass the inspection on Ellis Island, and they were deported. Many people were deported for medical reasons. Trachoma was by far the most common reason for deportation. Others were sent home because they had some sort of disability, and officials feared they would become a burden to society.

Frank Martucci, an interpreter at Ellis Island, said one of the saddest sights was when a woman came to America to join her husband or fiancé, but the man could not be located. Perhaps he had not received the letter immigration officials sent to him. Perhaps he had died. Perhaps he had moved. Martucci said, "There was no way of soothing these heartbroken women, who had traveled thousands and thousands of miles, endured suffering and humiliation, and who had uprooted their lives only to find their hopes shattered at the end of the long voyage."

Steamships took the people who were deported back to the European ports from which they had come. Many had nothing to go back to. They had sold all they owned to buy the ticket to America. In some cases, some members of a family were admitted to America, while others were deported. Husbands were separated from wives, and parents separated from their children.

People facing deportation sometimes made desperate attempts to escape. Some tried to swim to shore. A few made it. Others were captured or drowned in the attempt. Ellis Island, the Island of Hope, was sometimes the Island of Tears.

SPOTLIGHT ON

Returning Home

Not everyone who returned to Europe was deported. Many immigrants chose to go back. Perhaps they had only wanted to be in America long enough to earn money to feed families back home. Perhaps they missed the old country and the loved ones they had left behind. People from southern Italy were the most likely to return home, with about 40 percent making the voyage back. Jewish people had the lowest rate of return, mainly because many had fled the pogroms and their homes had been destroyed.

CHAPTER 4

STEMMING THE TIDE

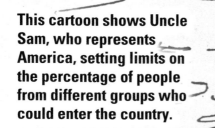

This cartoon shows Uncle Sam, who represents America, setting limits on the percentage of people from different groups who could enter the country.

IN 1897, ABOUT 180,000 immigrants passed through Ellis Island. By 1907, that number had grown to more than one million. It was the busiest year in Ellis Island's history. As the number of newcomers grew, some Americans became uneasy. Some worried about losing jobs to immigrants who would work for lower wages. Others were worried that the **ethnic** makeup of the country would be changed.

When Ellis Island first opened, Germans were the most common nationality to pass through its gates. Other northern Europeans such as Swedes and Irish were also common. By the turn of the century, immigrants were much more likely to be Italians and Russian Jews. Many Americans wanted the ethnic makeup of the country to remain the same. They began demanding restrictions on immigration.

Class No. 5   Serial Number 2674 Armeno-Turkish

վէ եեոի պին գոյուն վէ իւչ պին տէվէ վէ պէշ եիւզ ճիֆթ էօքիւզ
վէ պէշ եիւզ տիշի մէրքեպէ մալիք օլուպ՝ մէզ չոզ պէնատէերի
տախի վար իտի. վէ պու աատմ՝ շարգ էհալիսինին քեաֆֆէսին-
տէն պէօյիւք իտի:

His substance also was seven thousand sheep, and three
thousand camels, and five hundred yoke of oxen, and five hundred she asses, and a very great household; so that this man
was the greatest of all the men of the east.

(Job 1:3)

**Immigrants were given cards like this one to prove they could
read in their own language.**

Limits and Quotas

In 1917, Congress passed the Immigration Act. This
act said that all immigrants who were at least 16 years
old must pass a literacy, or reading, test in their own
language. Many immigrants came from poor villages
and had never been to school. They did not know how
to read, but they often found a way to make it look as if
they did.

One Armenian woman managed to pass the test
even though she could not read at all. She did this by
taking advantage of the fact that the immigration official
did not speak Armenian. "They handed her a book in
Armenian," recalled her daughter. "She said to my uncle,

'Now what do I do?' He says, in Armenian, of course, . . . 'Open a page and recite the Lord's Prayer in Armenian.' So she did. As soon as she did that, they passed her."

The Immigration Act did little to stem the flow of immigrants, so in 1921, Congress passed the **Quota** Act. This law limited the total number of immigrants entering the United States to about 350,000 a year. It also limited how many could come from each individual country. Further, the law stated that no more than 20 percent of a country's yearly total of immigrants could enter the United States in one calendar month.

Steamships began racing from Europe to New York early each month to ensure that their passengers would be admitted. Sometimes a ship arrived too late, after a country's quota had already been filled for

The Immigration and Quota Acts made it more difficult for many immigrants to pass inspection at Ellis Island.

The Quota Act resulted in many immigrants being deported as soon as they arrived in America.

that month. The desperate and bewildered passengers were refused entry. People who had given up everything to take a chance on America were forced to return to Europe. Henry Curran, the commissioner of Ellis Island, recalled watching them cry softly as they left. He wrote, "Day by day the barges took them from Ellis Island back to the ships again, back to the ocean, back to what?"

The National Origins Act

In 1924, Congress passed the most restrictive immigration law, the National Origins Act. This law reduced the number of immigrants allowed to about

This cartoon refers to the Statue of Liberty as a "dumping site" for immigrants.

A FIRSTHAND LOOK AT
AN IMMIGRATION CARTOON

In the early 1900s, debates over immigration restriction raged across the United States. At the time, political cartoons were very popular. They appeared in newspapers and magazines. Some cartoons showed fear and distrust of the newcomers. Others were sympathetic toward immigrants. See page 60 for a link to view a 1916 immigration cartoon that is critical of literacy tests.

After the National Origins Act, immigrants went through medical inspections before leaving home.

165,000, less than half of what the 1921 law allowed. The law's purpose was to try to preserve the older ethnic mix of the United States. Thus, it allowed many immigrants from countries in northern and western Europe, but very few from southern and eastern Europe, Africa, and the Middle East. People from Asia were not allowed to immigrate at all. The 1921 law had already limited the number of Italian immigrants to 42,000. The National Origins Act reduced that number to only 4,000.

The law also changed the way inspections were handled. No longer would immigrants travel thousands of miles and then be inspected at Ellis Island. Under the new law, immigrants were inspected before they left their home country. This prevented the agony of being refused entry and forced to make a return journey across the ocean.

The Island Grows Quiet

Once the inspections began overseas, very few people were brought to Ellis Island. Sometimes people would be detained at Ellis Island if they became sick on the ship or if they were caught trying to sneak into America without the proper inspection.

Ellis Island served as a **detention center** during World War II. In the war, the United States fought Germany, Italy, and Japan. Some citizens of these countries were held prisoner at Ellis Island. In addition, wounded American soldiers were treated at the island's hospital, and the Coast Guard sometimes used the island for training.

Irving Berlin

Among the millions of immigrants who poured through Ellis Island was a boy named Israel Baline. He grew up in poverty in Russia. When he was five years old, he watched his house burn to the ground in a pogrom. He and his parents and seven siblings soon escaped to New York City. On the rough streets of New York's Lower East Side, Israel became a singer and then began writing songs. He changed his name to Irving Berlin and soon wrote some of the most popular songs of the 20th century, including "Alexander's Ragtime Band" and his most famous song, "God Bless America."

Ellis Island is now home to an immigration museum.

Finally, in 1954, the last person being detained at Ellis Island, a Norwegian sailor named Arne Peterssen, was released. The immigration station was permanently closed.

Recalling the Stories

After the immigration station closed, people listened to the stories of their relatives who had made the journey across the ocean. They wanted to remember the experiences of the brave men, women, and children who had ventured to the United States to start a new life.

In 1965, President Lyndon Johnson named Ellis

Island a national monument. In the 1980s, the main building on Ellis Island was fixed up. It reopened in 1990 as the Ellis Island Immigration Museum.

Today, about two million people a year visit the museum to learn about the experiences of their parents and grandparents—or to relive their own youth. The museum exhibits explain why people left their homes and describes their difficult journey. The exhibits take visitors step by step through the Ellis Island inspection process. They show what life was like in steerage aboard the ships and while being detained on the island. The museum honors all those who left their homes in search of greater freedom and opportunity in America.

TODAY'S PERSPECTIVE

Through the years, Americans have grown increasingly interested in learning about their family histories. They yearn to know where their relatives came from and why they came to America. More than 100 million Americans, or one in every three, have relatives who entered the United States through Ellis Island.

Many people have turned to the records kept at Ellis Island to try to trace their family history. They search ship manifests and other records for clues about an ancestor's voyage to America.

What Happened Where?

Seattle
WA

MT

ND

OR

ID

SD

WY

NE

Angel
Island

NV

UT

CO

San
Francisco

CA

KS

The Angel Island Immigration Station The Angel Island Immigration Station in San Francisco Bay has been called the Ellis Island of the West. More than one million immigrants from Asia passed through Angel Island between 1910 and 1940.

AZ

NM

OK

Nogales

El Paso

TX

N
W   E
S

MEXICO

0   150   300 mi

0   150   300 km

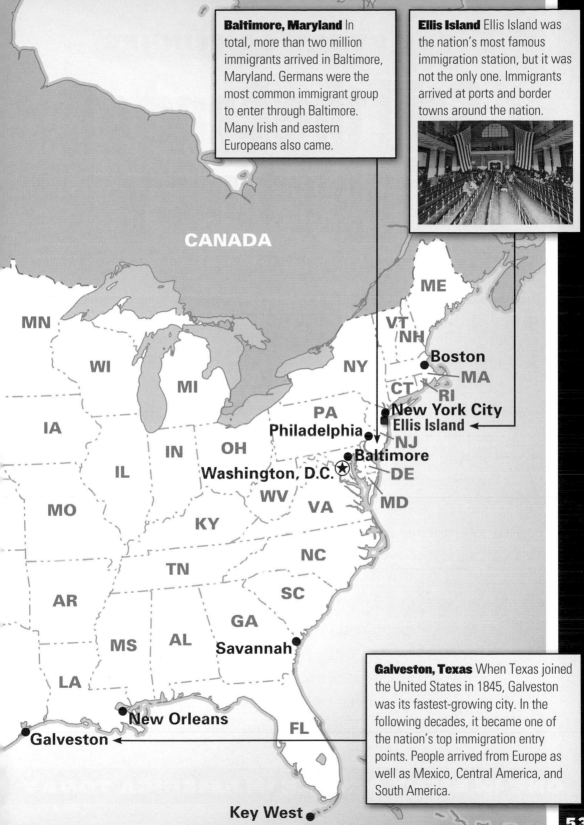

Baltimore, Maryland In total, more than two million immigrants arrived in Baltimore, Maryland. Germans were the most common immigrant group to enter through Baltimore. Many Irish and eastern Europeans also came.

Ellis Island Ellis Island was the nation's most famous immigration station, but it was not the only one. Immigrants arrived at ports and border towns around the nation.

CANADA

MN

WI

MI

IA

IN

OH

IL

MO

KY

AR

TN

MS

AL

LA

ME

VT

NH

NY

Boston

MA

CT

RI

PA

New York City

Philadelphia

Ellis Island

NJ

Baltimore

Washington, D.C.

DE

WV

VA

MD

NC

SC

GA

Savannah

New Orleans

FL

Galveston

Key West

Galveston, Texas When Texas joined the United States in 1845, Galveston was its fastest-growing city. In the following decades, it became one of the nation's top immigration entry points. People arrived from Europe as well as Mexico, Central America, and South America.

53

Still the Land of Opportunity

The United States is a nation of immigrants. Between 1820 and 2008, about 70 million people moved from another country to the United States. The immigrants who passed through Ellis Island were only one part of this mass movement that began when Europeans first set foot in North America.

Poor people around the world continue to look to the United States as a land of freedom and opportunity. Today's immigrants are less likely to be from Europe. Instead, they come from Mexico, China, India, Nigeria, El Salvador, and dozens of other countries.

As they did 100 years ago, Americans still argue over the impact of immigration on the nation. Some Americans claim that immigrants are changing the culture within the United States. Others point out that immigrants blend into and enrich the culture. Some people complain that immigrants take jobs from native-born Americans. Others point out that many new

ONE IN EIGHT PEOPLE IN AMERICA TODAY

immigrants take physically exhausting jobs that few native-born Americans want.

Whatever the outcome of the current immigration debate, Ellis Island remains a symbol of America's greatest ideals. For decades, the tiny island was the doorway to hope, opportunity, and freedom. At Ellis Island, America opened its arms to the poor and oppressed, offering them a better life.

Activists march, hoping to secure rights for recent immigrants.

WAS BORN IN A DIFFERENT COUNTRY.

INFLUENTIAL INDIVIDUALS

Max Factor (1875–1938) was a businessman born in Poland who came through Ellis Island in 1904. He founded the Max Factor cosmetics company.

Knute Rockne (1888–1931) was a football coach born in Norway who entered America through Ellis Island when he was five years old. He coached at the University of Notre Dame and is considered one of the greatest football coaches in history.

Irving Berlin (1888–1989) was a songwriter born in a part of Russia that is now Belarus. He went through Ellis Island in 1893. He wrote some of the most popular songs of the 20th century, including "God Bless America" and "Alexander's Ragtime Band."

Edward G. Robinson (1893–1973) was an actor born in Romania who passed through Ellis Island at age 10. He appeared in such films as *The Public Enemy* and *Little Caesar*.

Rudolph Valentino (1895–1926) was an actor born in Italy who passed through Ellis Island at age 18. He was one of the most popular actors of the silent film era, starring in such films as *The Sheik*.

Frank Capra (1897–1991) was a film director who was born in Italy and passed through Ellis Island in 1903. He directed many classic films, including *It's a Wonderful Life* and *It Happened One Night*.

Frank Capra

Claudette Colbert (1903–1996) was an actress born in France who passed through Ellis Island in 1906. She starred in such films as *Imitation of Life* and *It Happened One Night*.

Bob Hope (1903–2003) was a comedian born in England who passed through Ellis Island in 1907. He starred in many hugely popular films in the 1940s, including *Road to Morocco* and *My Favorite Blonde*.

Johnny Weissmuller (1904–1984) was a championship swimmer and actor born in Austria-Hungary, which is now Romania. He passed through Ellis Island as an infant. He won five Olympic gold medals and later gained fame playing Tarzan in the movies.

Isaac Asimov

Isaac Asimov (1920–1992) was a science fiction writer and scientist who was born in Russia. He passed through Ellis Island when he was three years old. He wrote more than 500 books, including *Foundation* and *I, Robot*.

TIMELINE

mid-1770s

Samuel Ellis buys the island.

1808

The U.S. government buys Ellis Island from the state of New York and begins construction of fortifications.

1891

Congress decides to use Ellis Island as an immigration station; Congress creates the Bureau of Immigration.

1921

The Quota Act of 1921 limits immigration to about 350,000 people per year and limits how many can come from each country.

1924

Congress passes the National Origins Act, reducing quotas for each nation so that only about 165,000 immigrants can enter the country.

1941–1946

German, Italian, and Japanese citizens are imprisoned at Ellis Island during and after World War II.

1892

The immigration station on Ellis Island opens.

1907

Ellis Island processes 1,004,756 immigrants, the most in its history.

1917

The Immigration Act is passed, requiring that immigrants age 16 and older be able to read in their own language before being admitted to the United States.

1954

The immigration station at Ellis Island closes.

1965

President Lyndon Johnson makes Ellis Island a national monument.

1990

The Ellis Island Immigration Museum opens.

LIVING HISTORY

Primary sources provide firsthand evidence about a topic. Witnesses to a historical event create primary sources. They include autobiographies, newspaper reports of the time, oral histories, photographs, and memoirs. A secondary source analyzes primary sources, and is one step or more removed from the event. Secondary sources include textbooks, encyclopedias, and commentaries.

Annie Moore's Name on a Ship's Manifest
Annie Moore was the first immigrant registered at the Ellis Island Immigration Station. To view the manifest of the ship that brought her to America and to see original handwritten details about Annie, go to *http://en.wikipedia.org/wiki/File:Annie_Moore_Arrival.jpg*

Immigrants and the Statue of Liberty
An 1887 sketch entitled "New York — Welcome to the land of freedom — An ocean steamer passing the Statue of Liberty: Scene on the steerage deck" shows new immigrants as they approached the Statue of Liberty in New York Harbor. To view the original black-and-white illustration, go to *http://loc.gov/pictures/resource/cph.3b49155/*

An Immigrant's Eye Test
To view the types of buttonhook tools that immigration doctors used for eye tests, go to *www.nps.gov/elis/historyculture/collections.htm*

Immigration Cartoon
To view a 1916 cartoon entitled "The Americanese Wall," which is critical of the policy of administering literacy tests to new immigrants, go to *http://loc.gov/pictures/resource/cph.3b00563/*

RESOURCES

Books

Bial, Raymond. *Ellis Island: Coming to the Land of Liberty*. Boston: Houghton Mifflin, 2009.

Bierman, Carol. *Journey to Ellis Island: How My Father Came to America*. New York: Hyperion, 1998.

Hammerschmidt, Peter A. *History of American Immigration*. Philadelphia: Mason Crest, 2009.

Jango-Cohen, Judith. *Ellis Island*. New York: Children's Press, 2005.

Kallen, Stuart A. *Twentieth-Century Immigration to the United States*. Detroit: Thomson Gale, 2007.

Rebman, Renee C. *Life on Ellis Island*. San Diego, CA: Lucent, 2000.

Sandler, Martin W. *Island of Hope: The Story of Ellis Island and the Journey to America*. New York: Scholastic, 2004.

Wolfman, Ira. *Climbing Your Family Tree: Online and Off-Line Genealogy for Kids*. New York: Workman, 2002.

Web Sites

Ellis Island
www.ellisisland.org
Here you can search ships' records to find out when your own relatives arrived at Ellis Island and download copies of the actual ships' passenger lists.

Scholastic—Stories of Yesterday and Today: Immigration
http://teacher.scholastic.com/activities/immigration/index.htm
Discover what it means to come to the United States as an immigrant, and learn about the experience through graphs, charts, and tables. You can even take an interactive tour of Ellis Island.

GLOSSARY

contagious (kuhn-TAY-juhss) able to be passed by contact between people

deported (di-PORT-id) sent back to the country from which a person came

detained (di-TAYND) held or kept as if in prison

detention center (dee-TEN-shuhn SEN-tur) a place where people are held until released

ethnic (ETH-nik) concerning a shared culture and history

famine (FAM-uhn) a serious lack of food

fortifications (for-tuh-fi-KAY-shuhnz) structures built for defense

immigrant (IM-uh-gruhnt) someone who moves from one country to another and settles there permanently

immigration (im-uh-GRAY-shuhn) coming from abroad to live in another country

manifest (MAN-ih-fest) a list of passengers on a ship

persecution (pur-suh-KYOO-shuhn) the cruel and unfair treatment of a person because of that person's background, ideas, or beliefs

pogroms (po-GRUHMZ) organized massacres of particular groups of people

quota (KWOH-tuh) a fixed amount of something

steerage (STEER-uhj) the section of a ship for passengers paying the lowest fare

Page numbers in *italics* indicate illustrations.

ABOUT THE AUTHOR

Melissa McDaniel Melissa McDaniel is a writer and editor who has a bachelor's degree in history and a master's degree in library science. She has written books for young people on subjects ranging from the Industrial Revolution to Isaac Newton to life on the deep-sea floor. Though McDaniel grew up in Portland, Oregon, she now lives in New York City. She and her daughter, Iris, have enjoyed several trips to Ellis Island, and they always find it a moving and memorable experience.